4K Books Publishing
Waldorf, MD
www.4kbookspublishing.blogspot.com
Email: 4kbookspublishing@gmail.com

FROM DATA TO DOLLARS: USING AI TO MONETIZE YOUR BUSINESS

THE BENEFITS OF AI FOR MONETIZATION.

By Kwame Joseph

PROLOGUE

In the world of business, the ability to generate profits is the ultimate goal. As we move further into the digital age, technology has become an increasingly important tool for achieving this goal. Among the many technologies available, artificial intelligence (AI) has emerged as a powerful tool for monetizing businesses.

From data analysis to customer service, AI has the ability to optimize and automate many aspects of business operations. But as with any new technology, there are challenges and risks to consider. In this book, we will explore the world of AI monetization, examining how businesses can use AI to drive revenue and the potential challenges and risks they may encounter along the way.

Whether you are a business owner looking to optimize your operations, a marketer looking to improve your campaigns, or simply curious about the future of AI in business, this book will provide valuable insights and practical strategies for implementing AI to drive profits. Join us on this journey as we explore the exciting world of AI monetization.

"In the near future, AI will become a basic skill that everyone will need to know." - Andrew Ng, Founder of Google Brain and former VP and Chief Scientist at Baidu

CHAPTER 1

Introduction

Welcome to "From Data to Dollars: Using AI to Monetize Your Business." This book is designed to provide business owners, managers, and executives with a comprehensive understanding of how to leverage the power of artificial intelligence (AI) to drive profits and achieve sustainable growth. Whether you're new to AI or an experienced practitioner, this book will give you the knowledge and tools you need to succeed in today's fast-paced business environment.

Artificial intelligence (AI) has become an increasingly important tool for businesses looking to drive profits and gain a competitive advantage. However, the potential of AI is often not fully understood by entrepreneurs, investors, and business professionals. This book aims to provide a comprehensive guide to using AI to make money, with a focus on practical strategies and real-world examples.

The purpose of this book is to help readers understand the potential of AI for monetization, and provide practical guidance on how to apply it in real-world scenarios. We'll explore the many ways in which AI can be used to enhance customer experience, reduce costs, and increase revenue. We'll also examine the challenges and risks associated with AI monetization, and provide actionable steps for overcoming them.

From Data to Dollars: Using AI to Monetize Your Business.is intended for a broad audience, including business owners, executives, managers, and professionals in a variety of industries. Whether you're in retail, healthcare, finance, or any other sector, this book will provide you with the knowledge and insights you need to leverage AI for business success.

By reading this book, you can expect to learn the following:

- An understanding of what AI is, how it works, and its potential applications
- The benefits of using AI for business, and how it can drive profits
- Strategies and business models for monetizing AI, with real-world case studies
- The challenges and risks of AI monetization, including ethical considerations, legal and regulatory risks, and technical challenges
- An exploration of the future of AI monetization, including emerging technologies and trends that are likely to shape the future of AI

In terms of structure, this book is organized into seven chapters. Chapter 2 provides an overview of AI, including its key technologies and techniques. Chapter 3 explores the potential of AI for business and how it can drive profits. Chapter 4 focuses on monetizing AI, with real-world case studies and strategies for success. Chapter 5 examines the challenges and risks of AI monetization, including ethical considerations, legal and regulatory risks, and technical challenges. Chapter 6 looks ahead to the future of AI monetization, examining emerging technologies and trends that are likely to shape the future of AI. Finally, Chapter 7 provides a summary of the key points covered in the book and actionable steps for readers to implement AI for driving profits.

We hope you find this book informative and useful, and we look forward to helping you navigate the exciting and rapidly-evolving world of AI monetization. Additionally, in this chapter, we will explore the various benefits of using AI for monetization, including its ability to automate processes, increase efficiency, and improve decision-making. We will also discuss the ways in which AI can provide businesses with a competitive advantage, and how it has the potential to disrupt industries and create new opportunities for growth.

Furthermore, this book is designed for business leaders, entrepreneurs, and anyone interested in understanding the potential of AI for driving profits. Whether you are a seasoned executive or a new startup founder, this book will provide you with the knowledge and tools needed to effectively leverage AI for monetization.

By the end of this book, readers can expect to have a deep understanding of how AI can be used to drive profits, and the various strategies and techniques that can be employed for effective AI monetization. With the knowledge and insights gained from this book, readers will be equipped to confidently implement AI into their businesses and take advantage of the opportunities presented by this rapidly evolving technology.

CHAPTER 2

Understanding AI

Artificial intelligence (AI) is a rapidly evolving field that is poised to revolutionize the way we work and live. In this chapter, we will provide an explanation of what AI is, how it works, and its potential applications. We will cover key technologies and techniques used in AI, and describe different types of AI and their uses in various industries. Additionally, we will provide a brief history of AI development.

A Brief History of AI Development

The concept of artificial intelligence dates back to the early days of computing in the 1950s, when scientists and researchers began exploring the idea of machines that could perform tasks traditionally reserved for humans. In 1956, the term "artificial intelligence" was coined by computer scientist John McCarthy, who organized the Dartmouth Conference, widely considered the birthplace of AI.

In the decades that followed, AI development progressed slowly but steadily. Early AI systems were based on rule-based expert systems, which were designed to mimic the decision-making processes of human experts in specific domains such as medicine, finance, and law.

However, the limitations of rule-based systems soon became apparent, and researchers began exploring more sophisticated approaches to AI. In the 1980s and 1990s, machine learning algorithms were developed that enabled AI systems to learn from data and improve their performance over time.

Today, AI development is driven by advances in deep learning, natural language processing, and computer vision. These technologies have enabled AI systems to perform increasingly complex tasks, such as recognizing images, understanding natural language, and making predictions based on large datasets.

What is AI?

At its core, AI is about creating machines that can perform tasks that normally require human intelligence. These tasks include recognizing speech, understanding natural language, making decisions, and learning from experience.

AI systems are typically built using machine learning algorithms that enable them to learn from data and improve their performance over time. These algorithms are based on statistical models that can identify patterns in data and make predictions based on those patterns.

Key Technologies and Techniques in AI

There are a number of key technologies and techniques used in AI, including:

• Machine learning: A type of AI that enables systems to learn from data and improve their performance over time.

• Deep learning: A type of machine learning that uses neural networks to model complex patterns in data.

• Natural language processing (NLP): The ability of machines to understand and process human language.

• Computer vision: The ability of machines to recognize and interpret visual information, such as images and videos.

• Robotics: The use of robots and other machines to perform tasks traditionally performed by humans.

Types of AI and Their Uses in Various Industries

There are three main types of AI: narrow or weak AI, general or strong AI, and artificial super-intelligence (ASI). Most of the AI systems in use today are narrow AI, which are designed to perform specific tasks, such as playing chess or recognizing images. General AI, on the other hand, is designed to perform any intellectual task that a human can do, while ASI is a hypothetical form of AI that would surpass human intelligence in every way.

AI is being used in a wide range of industries, including healthcare, finance, retail, and manufacturing. Some common types of AI and their uses include:

• Predictive analytics: AI systems can analyze vast amounts of data to make predictions about future trends, such as customer behavior or market conditions.

• Personalization: AI can be used to personalize experiences for individual customers, such as recommending products or tailoring marketing messages.

• Fraud detection: AI systems can detect and prevent fraudulent activity in financial transactions or other areas.

• Image and speech recognition: AI systems can recognize and interpret images and speech, which can be useful in a variety of applications such as medical diagnosis or security.

AI has applications in a wide range of industries, including healthcare, finance, retail, and manufacturing. In healthcare, AI is being used to diagnose diseases, develop new treatments, and analyze medical images. In finance, AI is being used to analyze data and make investment decisions. In retail, AI is being used to improve the customer experience and personalize marketing efforts. And in manufacturing, AI is being used to optimize production processes and reduce waste.

Here's a list of relevant quotes from different industry professionals, academic, and researchers regarding the future AI.

- "In the near future, AI will become a basic skill that everyone will need to know." - Andrew Ng, Founder of Google Brain and former VP and Chief Scientist at Baidu

Explanation: As AI becomes more ubiquitous, it will become increasingly important for individuals and businesses to understand and utilize AI technology. This will create new opportunities for AI monetization, as businesses will need to invest in AI-based solutions to remain competitive, and individuals with AI skills will be in high demand.

- "AI is a transformational technology that has the potential to create enormous value for businesses and society." - McKinsey Global Institute report on AI's potential value across industries

Explanation: As businesses and society increasingly adopt AI-based solutions, there will be a growing demand for AI monetization strategies. This could include developing AI-based products or services, investing in AI companies, or leveraging AI technology to improve operational efficiency and generate cost savings.

- "AI can provide companies with a significant competitive advantage by enabling them to make better decisions and drive innovation." - Forrester Research report on the impact of AI on business performance

Explanation: AI can enable companies to gain a competitive advantage by providing them with insights and analysis that

would be difficult or impossible for humans to generate on their own. This can drive innovation, reduce costs, and improve customer experiences, all of which can contribute to increased revenue and profitability.

- "As AI technology continues to improve, it will enable new applications and opportunities for monetization that we haven't even imagined yet." - Fei-Fei Li, Co-Director of the Stanford Institute for Human-Centered Artificial Intelligence

Explanation: As AI technology continues to advance, it will create new opportunities for monetization that are not yet possible. For example, new AI-based products and services may emerge, or AI technology may enable new business models that were previously impractical.

- "AI can help companies optimize pricing and revenue management, leading to increased profits." - Gartner report on the potential of AI for revenue management

Explanation: AI can enable companies to optimize pricing and revenue management by analyzing vast amounts of data to identify patterns and trends. This can enable businesses to make more informed pricing decisions, improve demand forecasting, and better manage inventory levels, all of which can lead to increased profits.

- "AI-powered chatbots can significantly reduce customer service costs and improve customer satisfaction." - Juniper Research report on the potential of chatbots

Explanation: Chatbots powered by AI technology can help businesses save on customer service costs by automating common tasks, such as answering frequently asked questions or processing routine transactions. This can improve operational efficiency while also providing customers with faster and more personalized service, leading to increased satisfaction and loyalty.

- "AI has the potential to revolutionize healthcare, creating new monetization opportunities for AI-based healthcare solutions." - PwC report on the impact of AI on healthcare

Explanation: AI has the potential to transform healthcare by improving patient outcomes, increasing operational efficiency, and reducing costs. This can create new monetization opportunities for AI-based healthcare solutions, such as diagnostic tools, personalized treatment recommendations, or predictive analytics to improve patient outcomes.

- "AI can help companies detect fraud and other types of financial crime, leading to cost savings and improved regulatory compliance." - KPMG report on the potential of AI for financial services

Explanation: AI can enable businesses to identify patterns and anomalies in large datasets that may indicate fraudulent activity or other types of financial crime. This can help businesses save on the costs associated with fraud and also ensure compliance with regulatory requirements, leading to increased revenue and profitability.

- "AI can help businesses develop more effective marketing strategies by providing insights into customer behavior and preferences." - McKinsey & Company report on the impact of AI on marketing

Explanation: AI can enable businesses to analyze vast amounts of data to gain insights into customer behavior and preferences. This can help businesses develop more effective marketing strategies by targeting the right customers with the right messages at the right time, leading to increased revenue and profitability.

- "AI can help businesses reduce supply chain costs by optimizing logistics, inventory management, and production planning." - Accenture report on the potential of AI for supply chain management

Explanation: AI can enable businesses to optimize supply chain management by analyzing vast amounts of data to identify patterns and trends. This can help businesses reduce costs by improving logistics, inventory management, and production planning, leading to increased efficiency and profitability.

What are the potential applications of AI?

AI has the potential to revolutionize several industries, from healthcare to finance to manufacturing. In healthcare, AI can be used to analyze medical images and help diagnose diseases, while in finance, it can be used to detect fraud and make investment decisions. In manufacturing, AI can be used to optimize production processes and improve product quality.

Overall, AI has the potential to bring significant benefits to businesses that are willing to invest in it. In the following chapters, we'll explore how AI can be used to drive profits and provide practical tips and strategies for businesses looking to incorporate AI into their operations.

AI has the potential to revolutionize numerous industries, from healthcare to finance, manufacturing to transportation. In healthcare, AI can be used to improve diagnosis accuracy, drug discovery, and patient outcomes. In finance, AI can be used for fraud detection, risk management, and investment decision-making. In manufacturing, AI can be used to optimize production processes and reduce downtime. In transportation, AI can be used for route optimization, predictive maintenance, and autonomous driving.

However, as with any technology, there are potential negative effects of AI as well. One concern is job displacement, as AI and automation may replace human workers in certain tasks. Another concern is the potential for bias and discrimination in AI systems, as they are only as unbiased as the data they are trained on. There are also concerns around privacy and data security, as AI systems rely heavily on large amounts of data.

Despite these potential negative effects, the benefits of AI are numerous, and it has the potential to drive significant progress and innovation in various industries. It is important for businesses to carefully consider the potential risks and benefits of AI before implementing it, and to ensure that it is used ethically and responsibly.

While AI has the potential to bring about many positive changes, it is also important to consider the negative effects it may have on society. Some of the potential negative impacts of an AI future include:

• Job displacement: AI has the potential to automate many jobs, which could lead to widespread job displacement and unemployment.

•   Bias and discrimination: AI algorithms may perpetuate and even amplify bias and discrimination, particularly if they are based on biased data or are not designed to account for diversity.

•   Privacy concerns: As AI collects and analyzes vast amounts of data, there are concerns about privacy and the potential misuse of personal information.

•   Security risks: AI systems can be vulnerable to cyberattacks, and their use in critical systems such as healthcare or transportation could have serious consequences if they are compromised.

•   Ethical concerns: The use of AI in areas such as autonomous weapons, surveillance, and decision-making raises ethical concerns about accountability, transparency, and the potential for harm.

•   Dependence on technology: As we become increasingly reliant on AI systems, there are concerns about our ability to function without them and the potential impact of system failures or malfunctions.

It is important to address these concerns and work towards solutions that ensure the benefits of AI are balanced with the potential risks and negative impacts.

CHAPTER 3

AI for Business

Artificial intelligence has the potential to revolutionize the way businesses operate. From enhancing customer experience to reducing costs and increasing revenue, AI can drive significant profits for companies across industries. In this chapter, we will explore the potential of AI for business and examine successful AI implementations.

Customer Experience

One of the most significant benefits of AI for businesses is its ability to enhance customer experience. AI-powered chatbots, for example, can provide customers with quick and efficient support, 24/7, which can lead to increased satisfaction and loyalty. In addition, personalized recommendations and targeted marketing campaigns can be created using AI algorithms, which can improve customer engagement and drive sales.

In today's world, customers demand a seamless and personalized experience when interacting with businesses.

AI has the potential to significantly enhance the customer experience by providing personalized recommendations, predictive insights, and 24/7 support. For instance, AI-powered chatbots can help customers get quick answers to their queries without having to wait for a human agent. AI can also analyze customer data to provide recommendations on products or services that customers are likely to be interested in based on their previous purchases or browsing history.

In the future, the use of AI in customer experience is expected to evolve even further. AI-powered virtual assistants will become more intelligent and personalized, using data from multiple sources such as social media, online browsing, and purchase history to provide tailored recommendations and support. For example, a customer could interact with an AI-powered virtual assistant to get personalized fashion recommendations based on their body type, style preferences, and past purchases.

As AI becomes more ubiquitous, it is likely that customers will evolve to rely on it more heavily. Customers may become accustomed to receiving personalized recommendations and support from AI, and may come to expect these features from businesses. In fact, it's possible that customers may not even consider doing business with companies that don't use AI to provide a personalized and seamless experience.

However, it's important to note that there are potential drawbacks to relying too heavily on AI for customer experience. Customers may feel like their privacy is being violated if companies collect too much data about them without their consent. Additionally, customers may become frustrated if they are not able to speak with a human agent when they need more in-depth support or have a complex issue that requires a human touch.

Overall, AI has the potential to revolutionize the customer experience, providing personalized and seamless interactions that can drive customer loyalty and satisfaction. However, businesses must be mindful of the potential risks and drawbacks of relying too heavily on AI and must strike a balance between automation and human touch to ensure that their customers are truly happy.

Cost Reduction

AI can also be used to reduce costs for businesses. For example, by automating repetitive tasks, such as data entry and analysis, companies can reduce the need for manual labor and save time and money. Additionally, predictive maintenance systems can be used to detect equipment failures before they occur, minimizing downtime and reducing repair costs.

In today's fast-paced business environment, companies are constantly looking for ways to reduce costs and increase profits. AI has proven to be an effective tool for achieving these goals. AI can analyze large amounts of data, identify patterns and trends, and provide valuable insights that can help businesses make better decisions.

One of the most significant benefits of using AI for cost reduction is that it can automate repetitive and time-consuming tasks. For example, in the manufacturing industry, AI can be used to automate quality control inspections, reducing the need for human inspectors and saving time and money.

AI can also be used to optimize supply chain management. By analyzing data on inventory levels, demand forecasts, and production schedules, AI can help businesses make more efficient use of their resources, reduce waste, and improve overall supply chain performance.

In terms of increasing profits, AI can help businesses identify new revenue streams and opportunities for growth. For example, AI can analyze customer data to identify patterns and trends in purchasing behavior, allowing businesses to tailor their marketing strategies and product offerings to better meet customer needs.

However, relying too heavily on AI for cost reduction and profit generation can also have its downsides. AI requires a significant investment in technology and training, which can be costly for businesses. Additionally, there is a risk of over-reliance on AI, which can lead to complacency and a lack of creativity in decision-making.

It's important for businesses to strike a balance between relying on AI for cost reduction and profit generation and retaining human expertise and creativity in decision-making. By doing so, businesses can maximize the benefits of AI while avoiding its potential pitfalls.

Revenue Generation

AI can also drive revenue growth for businesses. By leveraging data analytics and machine learning, companies can gain insights into customer behavior and preferences, which can inform product development and marketing strategies. In addition, AI can be used to optimize pricing strategies, predicting demand and setting prices accordingly, leading to increased revenue.

AI is already being used in various industries to enhance customer experience. For example, chatbots can provide 24/7 customer support, analyze customer data to provide personalized recommendations, and even process customer orders. In the future, AI has the potential to revolutionize customer experience even further by allowing for more intuitive, personalized interactions between customers and businesses.

One possible application of AI in customer experience is through the use of virtual assistants or digital concierges. These AI-powered tools can help customers navigate through complex product catalogs or service menus, provide recommendations based on their browsing history and preferences, and even help with purchase decisions.

Furthermore, AI can also help businesses anticipate customer needs and provide proactive service. For instance, predictive analytics can analyze customer behavior and provide personalized offers and recommendations before a customer even realizes they need them. This type of proactive service can not only enhance the customer experience but also increase customer loyalty and retention.

There are several pros and cons to relying on AI to drive revenue generation in a business.

Pros:

- AI can help identify new revenue streams and opportunities that may not have been apparent to human decision-makers.
- AI can quickly analyze large amounts of data to identify patterns and trends that can inform revenue-generating strategies.
- AI-powered personalization can improve the customer experience and lead to increased sales and revenue.
- AI can automate repetitive tasks, freeing up employees to focus on revenue-generating activities.
- AI can help businesses to better target their marketing efforts, leading to increased revenue.

Cons:

- AI may not be able to fully replicate the creativity and intuition of human decision-makers, potentially limiting the scope of revenue-generating strategies.
- The accuracy of AI predictions and recommendations may be limited by the quality and quantity of the data it has been trained on.
- Relying too heavily on AI to drive revenue generation can lead to a loss of human touch in customer interactions, potentially impacting customer loyalty and satisfaction.
- AI is not a one-size-fits-all solution and may require significant customization and integration efforts to achieve optimal results.
- AI can be expensive to implement and maintain, potentially eating into the revenue generated by its use.

As AI continues to evolve, it's likely that the future customer will become even more dependent on AI for their daily lives. This means that businesses will need to continue to invest in AI-powered customer experience solutions in order to remain competitive and meet the evolving expectations of their customers.

There are many companies that are publicly known to generate revenue from AI. Here are some examples:

- Google (Alphabet Inc.)
- Microsoft
- IBM
- Amazon
- Facebook
- NVIDIA
- Intel
- Tesla
- Baidu
- Alibaba Group
- Tencent
- Salesforce
- SAP
- Oracle
- Siemens
- General Electric
- Honeywell
- Philips
- Samsung
- LG
- Canon
- Fujitsu
- Hitachi
- NEC
- Panasonic
- Toshiba
- Accenture
- Capgemini
- Deloitte

- KPMG
- PwC
- McKinsey & Company
- Boston Consulting Group
- Accenture
- Infosys
- Wipro
- Cognizant
- HCL Technologies
- Tata Consultancy Services
- Genpact
- DXC Technology
- Atos
- CGI
- NTT Data
- Fujitsu Services
- Robert Bosch
- Continental AG
- Denso
- ZF Friedrichshafen AG
- Samsung SDS

The most common aspect of AI that these 50 companies share is the ability to collect and analyze vast amounts of data in real-time. They use this data to create predictive models and personalized recommendations for their customers. Many of these companies also use AI to automate their business processes and streamline their operations, which leads to increased efficiency and cost savings. Additionally, these companies often invest heavily in research and development to improve their AI capabilities and stay ahead of the competition. By leveraging AI in these ways, they are able to gain a competitive edge and drive revenue growth.

Examples of Successful AI Implementations

There are many successful AI implementations across industries. For example, the airline industry has used AI to optimize flight scheduling and reduce delays, resulting in significant cost savings. The healthcare industry has also used AI to improve patient outcomes, with machine learning algorithms being used to diagnose diseases and identify treatment options. E-commerce giant Amazon has also successfully implemented AI in its recommendation engine, providing personalized product suggestions to customers and driving sales.

Here are some examples of successful AI implementations:

• **Netflix:** Netflix uses machine learning algorithms to personalize the content shown to each user based on their viewing history, preferences, and behaviors. This AI implementation has helped Netflix to retain its customers and attract new ones.

• **Amazon:** Amazon uses AI algorithms to offer personalized product recommendations and to optimize its supply chain management. These AI implementations have helped Amazon to increase its sales and reduce its operational costs.

• **Spotify:** Spotify uses machine learning algorithms to create personalized playlists for each user, based on their listening history and preferences. This AI implementation has helped Spotify to increase its user engagement and retention.

• **Google:** Google uses AI algorithms to personalize search results and to optimize its ad targeting. These AI implementations have helped Google to maintain its dominance in the search engine market and to generate significant revenue from advertising.

• **Uber:** Uber uses machine learning algorithms to predict rider demand and to optimize driver routes, leading to a more efficient and cost-effective transportation service. This AI implementation has helped Uber to increase its revenue and to expand its user base.

• **Tesla:** Tesla uses AI algorithms to optimize its autonomous driving features and to improve vehicle safety. These AI implementations have helped Tesla to differentiate itself in the highly competitive automotive market and to attract customers who value advanced technology.

• **Adobe:** Adobe uses AI algorithms to enhance its digital marketing and content creation tools, allowing users to create more engaging and effective campaigns. This AI implementation has helped Adobe to maintain its position as a leader in the digital media and marketing industry.

• **IBM:** IBM uses AI algorithms to offer advanced data analytics and cognitive computing services to businesses, helping them to optimize their operations and make data-driven decisions. This AI implementation has helped IBM to generate significant revenue from its enterprise customers.

These are just a few examples of successful AI implementations across different industries. AI has the potential to transform businesses in many ways, from improving customer experience to optimizing operations and increasing revenue. However, it is important for businesses to carefully consider the potential risks and challenges associated with AI implementation, including data privacy, bias, and regulatory compliance.

There are several factors that contributed to the successful implementation of AI by these companies. Here are a few examples:

• **Investment in talent:** Companies that are successful with AI often invest in building a team of experts with deep knowledge of machine learning and data science. This talent is critical in identifying and implementing the right AI solutions for the business.

• **Data quality:** High-quality data is essential for successful AI implementation. Companies that are able to collect, clean, and analyze large amounts of data are often better positioned to leverage AI for revenue generation, cost reduction, and customer experience improvement.

• **Collaboration:** Successful AI implementations often require collaboration between different teams and departments within a company. This can include IT, data science, marketing, and operations. When these teams work together effectively, they can identify and implement AI solutions that benefit the entire organization.

• **Experimentation:** AI is a rapidly evolving field, and successful companies are often willing to experiment with different approaches and technologies to find the best solutions for their needs. This experimentation can involve testing different algorithms, data sources, or business models to find the optimal AI implementation.

• **Focus on business outcomes:** Ultimately, successful AI implementations are those that generate real business value. Companies that are able to identify specific business problems that can be addressed with AI, and that measure the impact of their solutions, are often the most successful in generating revenue and reducing costs with AI.

Conclusion

AI has enormous potential for businesses, providing opportunities for enhanced customer experience, cost reduction, and revenue growth. In this chapter, we have explored the benefits of AI for business and provided examples of successful AI implementations. In the following chapters, we will dive deeper into specific industries and examine how AI can be applied in different contexts.

CHAPTER 4

Monetizing AI

Artificial Intelligence (AI) has emerged as a key driver of business innovation and growth, providing companies with powerful new tools for improving operations, enhancing customer experiences, and generating revenue. In this chapter, we will explore the different strategies and business models for monetizing AI, and provide case studies of successful AI monetization. We will also explain how businesses can leverage AI for competitive advantage.

Monetizing AI requires a strategic approach that takes into account the unique opportunities and challenges of this emerging technology. Here are ten different strategies for monetizing AI:

- Selling AI as a product: One of the simplest ways to monetize AI is to sell it as a product. For example, companies can sell AI-enabled software, hardware, or services, providing customers with tools to automate tasks, optimize processes, or make better decisions.

- Offering AI as a service: Another approach is to offer AI as a service, providing customers with access to AI capabilities through a subscription or pay-per-use model. For example, companies can offer AI-powered chatbots, recommendation engines, or predictive analytics as a service.

- Licensing AI technology: Companies can license their AI technology to other businesses or developers, earning royalties or licensing fees. This approach allows companies to monetize their AI while leveraging the expertise of others to create new products or services.

• Using AI to enhance existing products or services: By integrating AI into existing products or services, companies can create new revenue streams or increase customer loyalty. For example, a retail company can use AI to personalize product recommendations, increasing the chances of customers making a purchase.

• Developing new AI-enabled products or services: Companies can also develop new products or services that are enabled by AI, creating new revenue streams and competitive advantages. For example, a healthcare company can use AI to develop new diagnostics or treatment methods.

• Partnering with other companies to create AI-enabled solutions: Collaboration can be a powerful way to monetize AI, allowing companies to combine their expertise to create new solutions. For example, a technology company can partner with a healthcare provider to develop AI-enabled medical devices.

• Offering AI-enabled consulting services: Companies can offer consulting services that use AI to help clients solve complex problems, such as predicting market trends or identifying new business opportunities.

• Creating a marketplace for AI: Companies can create a marketplace for AI technology, allowing developers to sell their AI models or algorithms to other businesses. This approach creates a network effect, where the value of the marketplace increases as more participants join.

• Selling data generated by AI: AI generates vast amounts of data, and companies can monetize this data by selling it to other businesses or using it to create new products or services. For example, a logistics company can use AI to optimize delivery routes, generating valuable data that can be sold to other companies.

• Using AI to reduce costs: Finally, companies can use AI to reduce costs, increasing profit margins and improving their bottom line. For example, a manufacturing company can use AI to optimize production processes, reducing waste and improving efficiency.

While there are certainly many potential benefits to monetizing AI, there are also some potential negative outcomes that businesses should be aware of.

One of the most significant risks of monetizing AI is the potential for bias and discrimination. This can occur when the data used to train an AI model is biased or incomplete, which can lead to inaccurate predictions or decisions that unfairly impact certain groups of people. This can have serious consequences, both in terms of reputation and legal liability.

Another risk is the potential for over-reliance on AI, which can lead to reduced human oversight and decision-making. This can be particularly problematic in high-stakes environments, such as healthcare or finance, where errors or malfunctions could have serious consequences. Additionally, if AI is relied on too heavily, there is a risk that it may become a "black box" that is difficult to understand or audit, which can make it difficult to identify and address problems.

Finally, there is also the risk of competition and commoditization. As more businesses look to monetize AI, there is a risk that the market may become oversaturated, driving down prices and making it difficult for companies to differentiate themselves. This can be particularly challenging for smaller businesses or startups that may not have the resources to compete with larger, more established players.

Overall, while there are certainly many potential benefits to monetizing AI, businesses should be aware of these potential negative outcomes and take steps to mitigate them. This may involve investing in ethical and responsible AI development practices, ensuring that there is adequate human oversight and decision-making, and focusing on areas where AI can provide real value and differentiation.

In Chapter 4, we dive deep into the world of monetizing AI. We start by explaining the various business models and strategies that companies can use to monetize their AI. This includes selling AI software, offering AI-as-a-Service, creating new AI-powered products and services, and more. We also explore the key considerations and challenges businesses face when deciding on the best approach for monetizing their AI.

To bring these concepts to life, we provide 10 detailed case studies of successful AI monetization across various industries, such as healthcare, finance, and e-commerce. Each case study examines how the company used AI to drive revenue and create new opportunities for growth. For example, we might explore how a healthcare company used AI to improve patient outcomes while also creating new revenue streams, or how a financial institution leveraged AI to automate customer service and streamline operations.

Throughout the chapter, we emphasize the importance of understanding the value that AI can bring to a business and aligning the monetization strategy with the overall business goals. We also discuss the role of data in AI monetization, including the importance of data quality and ethics.

Our goal with this chapter is to provide readers with a comprehensive understanding of the various ways in which AI can be monetized, as well as the benefits and challenges of each approach. We hope to inspire entrepreneurs, investors, and business professionals to think creatively about how they can leverage AI for competitive advantage and drive profits.

Here are 20 vital things to consider when monetizing artificial intelligence:

- Identify the business problem: Before considering how to

monetize AI, it's essential to identify a specific business problem that AI can solve. This will ensure that the investment in AI is justified and targeted towards achieving specific goals.

• Understand the data: The effectiveness of AI is largely dependent on the quality of the data it's trained on. Businesses need to ensure they have access to high-quality data to maximize the potential of AI.

• Data governance: As businesses collect and use more data, it's essential to have a robust data governance framework to ensure compliance with privacy regulations and prevent misuse of data.

• Select the right AI model: Choosing the right AI model is crucial to achieving optimal results. Different models are suited for different tasks, and it's essential to select the right one for the task at hand.

• Evaluate the cost of AI: AI can be expensive to implement, and businesses need to evaluate the costs involved before committing to an AI strategy.

• Determine the return on investment (ROI): A clear understanding of the ROI for AI investments is crucial to justifying the expense and identifying areas for improvement.

• Develop a business model: There are different business models for monetizing AI, such as selling data or charging for AI-powered services. It's essential to choose the right model for the specific application.

• Intellectual property: AI can generate valuable intellectual property, and businesses need to understand their rights and obligations when developing AI models.

• Security: AI systems can be vulnerable to attacks, and businesses need to ensure that their AI systems are secure and protected from cyber threats.

• Explainability: AI systems can be complex, and it's essential to be able to explain how decisions are made to build trust and transparency with customers.

• Regulation: As AI becomes more prevalent, governments are starting to introduce regulations. Businesses need to stay up-to-date with regulations and ensure compliance.

• Talent acquisition: AI is a specialized field, and businesses need to attract and retain talent with the necessary expertise to implement AI solutions.

• Training and development: AI models need to be continually trained and updated to maintain accuracy and relevance. Businesses need to invest in ongoing training and development.

• Infrastructure: AI systems require specialized infrastructure, such as high-performance computing resources. Businesses need to ensure they have the necessary infrastructure in place to support their AI strategies.

• Ethical considerations: AI has the potential to impact society significantly, and businesses need to consider the ethical implications of their AI strategies.

• Partnership and collaboration: Building partnerships and collaborating with other businesses can help accelerate AI development and implementation.

• Customer acceptance: AI solutions need to be accepted by customers to be successful. Businesses need to consider how to build trust and communicate the benefits of AI to customers.

• User experience: AI solutions need to be designed with the user in mind to ensure a positive user experience and maximize adoption.

• Scalability: AI solutions need to be scalable to accommodate increasing amounts of data and users.

• Continuous improvement: AI models need to be continually improved to maintain accuracy and relevance. Businesses need to have a process in place for ongoing improvement and innovation.

These are just some of the vital things to consider when monetizing artificial intelligence. By taking a comprehensive and strategic approach, businesses can maximize the potential of AI and drive significant profits.

Successful AI monetization requires careful planning and execution, as well as a deep understanding of the opportunities and challenges of this emerging technology. In the following sections, we will provide case studies of successful AI monetization, and explain how businesses can leverage AI for competitive advantage.

CHAPTER 5
Challenges and Risks of AI Monetization

While the potential of AI for driving profits is significant, there are also various challenges and risks associated with monetizing AI. In this chapter, we will examine some of these challenges and risks and explore how businesses can address them.

Ethical Considerations

One of the biggest challenges associated with AI monetization is ethical considerations. AI is a powerful tool that can have significant impacts on individuals and society as a whole. Therefore, businesses must ensure that their AI applications are designed and used ethically. This means avoiding biases and ensuring transparency in decision-making processes.

Another important ethical consideration when it comes to AI monetization is the issue of bias. AI systems can inadvertently inherit and amplify biases present in the data used to train them. This can lead to discriminatory outcomes and potential harm to individuals or groups. Businesses must proactively address this issue by identifying and mitigating bias in their AI systems.

In addition to ethical considerations, there are also legal and regulatory risks associated with AI monetization. Many countries have developed or are developing regulatory frameworks to govern the use of AI, such as the General Data Protection Regulation (GDPR) in Europe and the California Consumer Privacy Act (CCPA) in the United States. Businesses must ensure that their

AI systems comply with relevant regulations and take steps to manage legal and reputational risks.

Finally, there are technical challenges associated with AI monetization. AI systems require vast amounts of data and computational resources, which can be costly to acquire and maintain. Additionally, the development and deployment of AI systems require specialized skills and expertise that may be difficult to find and retain. Businesses must carefully consider these challenges and plan accordingly when implementing AI monetization strategies.

Overall, while AI monetization can offer significant benefits, it is important for businesses to carefully consider the ethical, legal, and technical challenges and risks associated with this approach. By proactively addressing these issues, businesses can maximize the potential of AI while minimizing potential harm and negative impacts.

Legal and Regulatory Risks

Another challenge associated with AI monetization is legal and regulatory risks. Businesses must ensure that they comply with relevant laws and regulations, such as the General Data Protection Regulation (GDPR) and the California Consumer Privacy Act (CCPA). Failure to comply with these regulations can result in significant legal and financial consequences.

Technical Challenges

Technical challenges are also a consideration when it comes to monetizing AI. AI systems are complex, and businesses must ensure that their systems are reliable, secure, and scalable. They must also ensure that their systems are interoperable and can integrate with other systems as needed.

As businesses increasingly turn to AI to drive profits, they must grapple with a host of technical challenges. AI systems are complex, relying on advanced algorithms and large datasets to generate insights and make predictions. This complexity can lead to technical difficulties that require significant expertise and resources to resolve.

One key challenge is ensuring that AI systems are reliable, secure, and scalable. Reliability is critical for businesses that rely on AI to make critical decisions, such as in healthcare or finance. Any error in the AI system can have severe consequences, potentially causing harm to people or leading to significant financial losses. Ensuring the security of AI systems is also essential to protect sensitive data and intellectual property from theft or cyber attacks. Scalability is necessary to accommodate increasing data volumes and processing requirements as the business grows.

Another important consideration for businesses is ensuring that their AI systems are interoperable and can integrate with other systems as needed. AI is often integrated with other technologies such as cloud computing, big data, and the Internet of Things. Therefore, businesses must ensure that their AI systems can work seamlessly with other technologies to generate insights and drive profits.

What is General Data Protection Regulation (GDPR)?

The General Data Protection Regulation (GDPR) is a regulation that was adopted by the European Union (EU) in 2016 and became enforceable in May 2018. Its primary goal is to strengthen and unify data protection for all individuals within the EU, as well as to regulate the export of personal data outside of the EU.

The GDPR applies to all businesses that process personal data of EU citizens, regardless of where the business is located. It gives individuals greater control over their personal data and requires businesses to obtain explicit consent before collecting and processing their data. The regulation also establishes specific rights for individuals, including the right to access and correct their personal data, the right to erasure (also known as the "right to be forgotten"), and the right to data portability.

To comply with the GDPR, businesses must take appropriate technical and organizational measures to protect personal data and ensure that it is processed in a lawful, fair, and transparent manner. They must also appoint a data protection officer, conduct regular privacy impact assessments, and report any data breaches to the relevant supervisory authority within 72 hours.

The GDPR carries significant fines for non-compliance, with penalties of up to €20 million or 4% of a business's global annual revenue, whichever is greater.

What is California Consumer Privacy Act (CCPA)?

The California Consumer Privacy Act (CCPA) is a privacy law that took effect on January 1, 2020, in California, United States. The law provides California residents with certain rights regarding their personal information that is collected by businesses. The CCPA applies to for-profit businesses that collect California residents' personal information and meet certain criteria, such as having annual gross revenues over $25 million, or processing the personal information of 50,000 or more California residents, households, or devices annually. The CCPA requires businesses to provide clear and specific disclosures about the personal information they collect, the purposes for which it will be used, and the third parties with whom it will be shared. It also gives consumers the right to access, delete, and opt-out of the sale of their personal information, among other rights. The CCPA has significant implications for businesses operating in California and has served as a model for other states and countries in developing their own privacy laws.

As AI is increasingly being used for monetization, businesses need to ensure that they comply with relevant laws and regulations. Failure to comply with these regulations can lead to serious legal and financial consequences, damaging a business's reputation and bottom line. In this chapter, we will explore the legal and regulatory risks associated with AI monetization, and why it is important for businesses to be aware of them.

One of the biggest challenges for businesses is complying with the General Data Protection Regulation (GDPR) and the California Consumer Privacy Act (CCPA). The GDPR is a regulation that was enacted by the European Union to protect the privacy of its citizens. It applies to businesses that process personal data of EU citizens, regardless of where the business is located. The CCPA, on the other hand, is a state-level law in California that applies to businesses that collect personal data of California residents. Both the GDPR and the CCPA have strict requirements for data protection and privacy, and businesses that fail to comply with these regulations can face significant penalties.

In addition to complying with GDPR and CCPA, businesses must also ensure that their AI systems are transparent and explainable. This is particularly important when AI is used for decision-making, such as in credit scoring or hiring practices. The use of opaque AI systems can lead to bias and discrimination, and can also violate anti-discrimination laws.

Another legal and regulatory risk associated with AI monetization is intellectual property (IP) rights. AI models and algorithms are valuable intellectual property, and businesses must ensure that they have the appropriate licenses and permissions to use them. Additionally, businesses must ensure that their AI systems do not infringe on the IP rights of others.

In conclusion, businesses must be aware of the legal and regulatory risks associated with AI monetization. Compliance with GDPR and CCPA is critical, as failure to comply can lead to significant penalties. Businesses must also ensure that their AI systems are transparent, explainable, and do not violate IP rights. By proactively addressing these risks, businesses can reduce the potential legal and financial impact of AI monetization.

To address these technical challenges, businesses must invest in the necessary expertise and resources. This includes hiring skilled data scientists, software engineers, and IT professionals who can design and implement reliable, secure, and scalable AI systems. It also means investing in robust data infrastructure, such as cloud computing and big data solutions, to support the processing and storage of large datasets. By addressing these technical challenges, businesses can leverage AI to drive profits and gain a competitive advantage in their respective markets.

Privacy and Bias

Privacy is a significant concern when it comes to AI monetization. Businesses must ensure that they protect their customers' personal data and avoid violating their privacy rights. They must also be aware of potential biases in AI systems and work to mitigate these biases.

Privacy and bias are significant concerns when it comes to AI monetization. Businesses must ensure that they protect their customers' personal data and avoid violating their privacy rights. With the massive amount of data being collected and processed by AI systems, there is a greater risk of exposing personal information and violating privacy laws.

In addition to privacy concerns, there is also the issue of bias in AI systems. AI systems are only as good as the data they are trained on. If the data used to train the AI system is biased, then the resulting AI system will also be biased. This can have serious consequences, especially in areas like hiring, lending, and criminal justice, where biased AI systems can perpetuate existing discrimination.

To mitigate these biases, businesses should ensure that their data sets are diverse and representative of the population they are serving. They should also ensure that their AI models are regularly audited for bias and take steps to correct any biases that are identified.

In addition, businesses can implement privacy-enhancing technologies such as differential privacy, which helps to protect individual privacy while still allowing for useful insights to be drawn from the data. This can help to reduce the risk of violating privacy laws and protect customers' personal information.

Biases in AI systems can arise from a variety of sources, including biased data sets, biased algorithms, and biased human input. Here are 20 ways to mitigate biases in AI systems:

- Establish clear goals for the AI system
- Define the scope and limitations of the AI system
- Use diverse and representative data sets
- Conduct an audit of data sources to identify and address biases
- Train and test AI models on diverse data sets
- Monitor AI models for bias and correct as necessary
- Implement measures to ensure the accuracy of AI models
- Develop transparency and explainability measures for AI models
- Include ethical considerations in the design and implementation of AI systems
- Involve diverse stakeholders in the development and deployment of AI systems
- Use multiple perspectives and sources to evaluate AI systems
- Adopt an iterative approach to the development of AI systems
- Use feedback loops to continually improve AI systems
- Develop clear policies and procedures for the use of AI systems
- Ensure that AI systems are used for their intended purpose
- Regularly review and update AI systems to ensure they remain relevant and effective
- Use independent audits and evaluations to identify and address biases
- Provide training and education to users of AI systems
- Engage in dialogue with stakeholders about AI systems and

their impact
•   Promote diversity and inclusivity in the development and deployment of AI systems.

By adopting these practices, businesses can work to mitigate biases in their AI systems and ensure that they are fair, accurate, and reliable

Transparency

Transparency is a critical consideration when it comes to AI monetization because AI systems can be complex and difficult to understand. When businesses use AI, they must be able to explain how their systems work and how decisions are made. This is especially important in industries such as finance and healthcare, where decisions made by AI can have a significant impact on individuals.

Businesses must ensure that they are transparent about their AI systems and the decision-making processes they use. They should explain how their AI systems work, what data is used to train their models, and how their models make decisions. This level of transparency can help build trust with customers and stakeholders and can also help mitigate concerns around privacy and bias.

By being transparent, businesses can also identify potential issues with their AI systems and correct them before they cause harm. For example, if a model is found to be making biased decisions, the business can take steps to correct the bias and improve the model's accuracy.

In addition to building trust and mitigating risk, transparency can also be a competitive advantage for businesses. By being transparent about their AI systems, businesses can differentiate themselves from their competitors and showcase their commitment to ethical and responsible AI practices.

Here are 20 examples of how transparency can be a competitive advantage for businesses:

• Increases customer trust and loyalty: By being transparent about your AI systems, customers are more likely to trust your brand and become loyal customers.

• Enhances brand reputation: A transparent approach to AI can help build a positive brand reputation and improve brand perception.

• Attracts new customers: Customers are more likely to be attracted to businesses that are open and honest about their AI systems.

• Improves customer satisfaction: By being transparent about how AI is used to enhance customer experience, businesses can improve customer satisfaction.

• Builds stronger relationships with customers: Transparency can help businesses build stronger relationships with their customers.

• Reduces customer complaints and concerns: When customers understand how AI is used, they are less likely to have complaints or concerns.

• Demonstrates social responsibility: Transparency shows that a business is socially responsible and accountable.

• Helps to avoid legal and regulatory issues: By being transparent, businesses can ensure that they are compliant with legal and regulatory requirements.

• Builds employee trust and engagement: Transparency can help build trust and engagement among employees, which can lead to higher productivity and job satisfaction.

• Encourages collaboration and innovation: Transparency can foster collaboration and innovation, as employees are more likely to share ideas and work together when they understand how AI is being used.

- Helps businesses stand out from competitors: Transparency can be a unique selling point and help businesses differentiate themselves from competitors.

- Builds investor confidence: Investors are more likely to invest in businesses that are transparent about their AI systems and decision-making processes.

- Creates a more accountable culture: Transparency can create a culture of accountability, where employees are more likely to take responsibility for their actions and decisions.

- Improves decision-making: By being transparent about how decisions are made using AI, businesses can improve their decision-making processes.

- Increases efficiency: Transparency can help identify inefficiencies in AI systems, which can then be addressed and improved upon.

- Promotes ethical behavior: Transparency can promote ethical behavior and discourage unethical practices, as employees are more likely to be held accountable for their actions.

- Builds trust with stakeholders: Transparency can build trust with stakeholders, including shareholders, customers, and employees.

- Creates opportunities for feedback and improvement: By being transparent, businesses can invite feedback and suggestions for improvement from stakeholders.

- Helps businesses stay ahead of the curve: Transparency can help businesses stay ahead of the curve in terms of emerging AI technologies and trends.

- Builds a culture of learning: Transparency can create a culture of learning, where employees are encouraged to learn more about AI and how it can be used to drive business success.

Overall, transparency is a critical component of AI monetization. Businesses must ensure that they are open and honest about their AI systems and the decision-making processes they use in order to build trust with their customers and stakeholders, mitigate risk, and gain a competitive advantage.

Conclusion

In conclusion, there are various challenges and risks associated with AI monetization. These challenges and risks can be addressed by ensuring that AI applications are designed and used ethically, complying with relevant laws and regulations, addressing technical challenges, and prioritizing privacy and transparency. By doing so, businesses can leverage the potential of AI while minimizing risks and maximizing benefits.

CHAPTER 6
The Future of AI Monetization

As AI continues to evolve and expand its applications, the future of AI monetization is a topic of increasing interest and importance. This chapter explores some of the emerging trends and technologies that are likely to shape the future of AI and how businesses can prepare for the changes to come.

1. Increasing adoption of AI technologies

As AI technologies become more accessible and affordable, we can expect to see a surge in their adoption across different industries. This will drive increased competition in the AI market, creating new opportunities and challenges for businesses. Companies that can effectively leverage AI will have a significant advantage over those that do not.

The future of AI monetization looks bright as the adoption of AI technologies is expected to surge in the coming years. One of the reasons for this is the increasing accessibility and affordability of AI technologies. Many businesses, particularly small and medium-sized enterprises, are beginning to see the potential benefits of AI and are investing in these technologies to gain a competitive edge.

As AI technologies become more mainstream, we can expect to see them being used in a wider range of industries, including healthcare, finance, retail, and manufacturing. For instance, AI-powered diagnostic tools are becoming increasingly common in healthcare, while financial institutions are using AI to detect fraud and improve customer experience.

The adoption of AI technologies is also likely to drive innovation and create new business models. For example, companies may begin to offer AI-based services and solutions, such as AI-powered chatbots and virtual assistants, as a way to differentiate themselves in the market.

However, with the increasing adoption of AI technologies also comes new challenges and risks. Businesses will need to ensure that they are using AI ethically and responsibly, and that they are addressing issues such as bias, privacy, and transparency. In addition, there will be a growing demand for skilled AI professionals who can design, develop, and maintain AI systems.

Despite these challenges, the future of AI monetization looks promising. As AI technologies become more advanced and accessible, we can expect to see businesses leveraging these technologies to drive profits and gain a competitive edge. It is important for businesses to stay ahead of the curve and to invest in AI technologies to remain competitive in today's fast-paced and rapidly changing business landscape.

2. Focus on ethical and responsible AI

As AI becomes more integrated into our daily lives, there is a growing concern about the potential ethical implications of its use. Companies that prioritize ethical and responsible AI will be better positioned to earn the trust and loyalty of their customers. This will be particularly important in industries such as healthcare and finance, where the stakes are high.

As AI becomes more integrated into our daily lives, there is a growing concern about the potential ethical implications of its use. This has led to a growing emphasis on ethical and responsible AI, which involves ensuring that AI systems are developed, implemented, and used in a manner that aligns with ethical principles and values.

Businesses that prioritize ethical and responsible AI are better positioned to earn the trust and loyalty of their customers. Consumers are increasingly aware of the potential negative consequences of AI and want to be assured that businesses are taking appropriate measures to ensure that AI is used in a responsible and ethical manner. By prioritizing ethical and responsible AI, businesses can demonstrate their commitment to ethical practices and earn the trust and loyalty of their customers.

One of the key considerations in ethical and responsible AI is ensuring that AI systems are developed and used in a manner that is consistent with human values and rights. This includes ensuring that AI systems do not discriminate against individuals on the basis of factors such as race, gender, or religion. It also involves ensuring that AI systems are transparent and explainable, meaning that they can be understood and their decisions can be justified.

Another consideration is ensuring that AI systems are secure and protect personal data. As AI systems become more integrated into our lives, there is a growing risk that they could be used to collect, store, and analyze personal data in ways that violate privacy rights. Businesses must ensure that they implement appropriate measures to protect personal data and prevent unauthorized access to AI systems.

Finally, businesses must ensure that AI systems are used in a manner that aligns with broader ethical principles and values. This includes ensuring that AI systems are not used to harm individuals or society as a whole. For example, businesses must ensure that they do not use AI to manipulate individuals or to spread misinformation.

In conclusion, prioritizing ethical and responsible AI is critical for businesses that want to succeed in the future of AI monetization. By demonstrating a commitment to ethical practices, businesses can earn the trust and loyalty of their customers, mitigate legal and regulatory risks, and ensure that AI is used in a manner that aligns with human values and rights.

3. Continued development of natural language processing (NLP)

Natural language processing (NLP) is an AI technology that enables computers to understand human language and respond accordingly. As NLP continues to develop, we can expect to see significant advancements in areas such as voice assistants, chatbots, and customer service. Companies that can effectively implement NLP will be able to provide more personalized and efficient service to their customers.

NLP works by analyzing and processing the structure and meaning of natural language text or speech. The process typically involves several stages, including:

• Tokenization: This involves breaking down the text into individual units, such as words or phrases, which are referred to as tokens.
• Part-of-speech (POS) tagging: This involves assigning a grammatical tag to each token, such as noun, verb, or adjective.
• Named entity recognition (NER): This involves identifying and categorizing entities in the text, such as people, organizations, and locations.
• Parsing: This involves analyzing the grammatical structure of the text, including identifying sentence boundaries, subjects, and objects.
• Sentiment analysis: This involves analyzing the tone or sentiment expressed in the text, such as positive, negative, or neutral.
• Language generation: This involves using the processed text to generate new text, such as in the case of chatbots or language translation.

NLP systems typically use machine learning algorithms, such

as deep learning, to analyze and process natural language. These algorithms are trained on large datasets of annotated text, which allows them to learn patterns and relationships in the data and make predictions about new text.

Advancements in NLP technology have led to significant improvements in areas such as voice assistants, chatbots, and customer service. For example, voice assistants such as Amazon's Alexa and Apple's Siri use NLP to understand spoken commands and respond appropriately. Chatbots, which are computer programs that can simulate human conversation, use NLP to understand and respond to user inputs. In customer service, NLP can be used to analyze customer feedback and sentiment to improve products and services.

Overall, NLP is an important area of AI that has the potential to revolutionize the way we interact with machines and make use of natural language data.

Natural Language Processing (NLP) is a subset of AI that focuses on enabling machines to understand, interpret, and interact with human language. As more and more businesses adopt AI technologies, the importance of NLP will only continue to grow. In this section, we will explore why the continued development of NLP is important and provide 20 examples of significant advancements in areas such as voice assistants, chatbots, and customer service.

Why is the Continued Development of NLP Important?

•	Better Communication with Customers: NLP can help businesses to communicate more effectively with their customers. With NLP, machines can understand natural language queries and respond appropriately, making customer interactions more efficient and satisfying.

•	Improved Customer Service: As machines become better at understanding and interpreting natural language, they can be used to automate customer service tasks. This can help businesses to reduce costs and improve the quality of customer service.

• Increased Efficiency: NLP can help businesses to automate routine tasks such as data entry, freeing up employees to focus on more strategic tasks.

• Improved Search Capabilities: With NLP, machines can better understand the intent behind search queries, enabling them to provide more accurate and relevant results.

• Enhanced Content Creation: NLP can help businesses to automate the process of creating content such as product descriptions and blog posts. This can save time and improve the quality of content.

• Better Personalization: NLP can help businesses to personalize their marketing messages based on customer data, improving the relevance and effectiveness of those messages.

• Increased Accessibility: NLP can help to make products and services more accessible to people with disabilities. For example, voice assistants can be used by people with visual impairments to access information and services.

• Enhanced Fraud Detection: NLP can be used to detect fraudulent activities such as phishing attacks and identity theft.

• Improved Sentiment Analysis: NLP can help businesses to analyze customer feedback and sentiment, enabling them to make more informed decisions about product development and marketing.

• Enhanced Language Translation: NLP can be used to improve language translation services, making it easier for businesses to communicate with customers around the world.

• Better Voice Assistants: With advancements in NLP, voice assistants such as Siri and Alexa are becoming more sophisticated and better able to understand and respond to natural language queries.

• Improved Chatbots: Chatbots are becoming more common in customer service, and advancements in NLP are making them more effective at understanding and responding to customer queries.

• More Natural Conversations: As machines become better at

understanding natural language, conversations with machines will become more natural and intuitive.

•   Improved Information Retrieval: NLP can help businesses to more effectively retrieve information from large datasets, enabling them to make more informed decisions.

•   Better Speech Recognition: With advancements in NLP, machines are becoming better at recognizing and interpreting different accents and dialects.

• Enhanced Personal Assistants: NLP can be used to create more sophisticated personal assistants, capable of performing a wider range of tasks and responding to more complex queries.

•   Improved Language Understanding: As machines become better at understanding natural language, they will be better able to understand the nuances of language, including sarcasm and humor.

• More Accurate Language Translation: With advancements in NLP, language translation services are becoming more accurate, enabling businesses to communicate more effectively with customers around the world.

• Better Data Analysis: NLP can be used to analyze large datasets of unstructured data such as customer feedback and social media posts, enabling businesses to gain insights that would be difficult to obtain through manual analysis.

•   Enhanced User Experience: With advancements in NLP, machines will be better able to understand and respond to user needs, creating a more satisfying and personalized user experience.

4. Increased use of AI in cybersecurity

As cyber threats continue to evolve and become more sophisticated, AI will play an increasingly important role in cybersecurity. AI-powered security solutions will be able to detect and respond to threats in real-time, providing a critical layer of protection for businesses.

As cyber threats continue to increase in frequency, complexity, and severity, cybersecurity has become an essential aspect of any business's operations. Hackers are using increasingly sophisticated methods to penetrate computer systems, steal sensitive data, and cause damage. Organizations must constantly adapt and strengthen their defenses to stay ahead of the ever-evolving threat landscape. This is where the power of artificial intelligence (AI) can be utilized to enhance cybersecurity.

AI-powered security solutions can provide a critical layer of protection for businesses, helping them detect and respond to threats in real-time. These solutions can be used to identify and block malicious activities, analyze large amounts of data to detect anomalies and patterns, and automate incident response. Additionally, AI can help cybersecurity professionals manage the sheer volume of data generated by security systems, reducing the workload on human analysts and freeing them to focus on more complex tasks.

One of the key benefits of AI-powered security solutions is their ability to learn and adapt over time. Machine learning algorithms can analyze vast amounts of data to identify patterns and anomalies, and use this information to improve their ability to detect and respond to threats. As new threats emerge, AI can quickly adapt to these new challenges, providing a proactive approach to cybersecurity that can help prevent attacks before they occur.

AI can also be used to enhance the accuracy and speed of threat detection and response. By analyzing large amounts of data in real-time, AI-powered security solutions can quickly identify and respond to threats, reducing the time it takes to detect and respond to an incident. This can significantly reduce the impact of an attack and minimize the risk of data loss or other damages.

Another significant advantage of AI-powered security solutions is their ability to identify and respond to insider threats. Insider threats are becoming increasingly common, as employees or contractors may intentionally or unintentionally compromise data security. AI can help detect suspicious behavior, such as unauthorized access to sensitive data or attempts to extract data from the network. This can help identify potential insider threats before they cause significant damage.

In conclusion, the use of AI in cybersecurity is becoming increasingly important as cyber threats continue to evolve and become more sophisticated. AI-powered security solutions can provide a critical layer of protection for businesses, detecting and responding to threats in real-time, improving accuracy and speed of detection, and reducing the risk of data loss or other damages. As businesses continue to embrace AI for cybersecurity, it is important to ensure that these solutions are developed and implemented with the highest level of security and ethical considerations in mind.

5. Collaboration between humans and AI

As AI technologies continue to advance, there will be an increasing need for collaboration between humans and machines. This will require a new approach to work and education, as humans and machines work together to solve complex problems and create new opportunities.

Overall, the future of AI monetization is bright, with numerous opportunities for businesses that can effectively leverage AI technologies. However, it will also be important to address the ethical and technical challenges that come with the territory. By staying ahead of the curve and preparing for the changes to come, businesses can position themselves for success in the exciting and rapidly evolving world of AI.

CHAPTER 7

Conclusion

Throughout this book, we've explored the vast potential of artificial intelligence (AI) for driving profits in businesses of all kinds. We've seen how AI can be used to enhance customer experience, reduce costs, and increase revenue. We've also discussed various strategies and business models for monetizing AI and explored real-life case studies of successful AI implementations across different industries. In this concluding chapter, we'll summarize the key points covered in the book and provide actionable steps for readers to implement AI for driving profits. We'll also offer final thoughts on the potential of AI for monetization and its impact on businesses.

Key Takeaways

Before we delve into the actionable steps for AI monetization, let's summarize some of the key takeaways from the previous chapters:

- AI is a rapidly evolving technology that has the potential to transform various industries.

- There are different types of AI, including machine learning, deep learning, and natural language processing, each with its own applications and limitations.

- Businesses can leverage AI to enhance customer experience, reduce costs, and increase revenue through various strategies, including automation, personalization, and predictive analytics.

• There are different business models for monetizing AI, including selling AI-based products and services, licensing AI technology, and using AI to optimize business processes.

• Successful AI monetization requires a combination of technical expertise, domain knowledge, and a deep understanding of customer needs and expectations.

• However, AI monetization also comes with various challenges and risks, including ethical considerations, legal and regulatory risks, and technical challenges such as bias and transparency.

Actionable Steps for AI Monetization

Now that we've reviewed some of the key takeaways from the book let's explore some actionable steps for implementing AI monetization in your business.

• Identify business opportunities for AI
The first step is to identify areas of your business where AI can be used to drive profits. This can include identifying customer pain points and areas where automation or personalization can enhance the customer experience, as well as optimizing business processes and reducing costs through predictive analytics.

• Build a team with the right skills
Successful AI monetization requires a team with the right skills and expertise, including data scientists, software engineers, and domain experts. Building a team with the right combination of skills can be challenging, but it's critical for the success of your AI initiatives.

• Develop a roadmap for AI implementation
Once you've identified business opportunities for AI and built a team with the right skills, it's time to develop a roadmap for AI implementation. This should include a timeline for different phases of the implementation process, a clear definition of

success metrics, and a plan for monitoring and optimizing AI performance.

- Address ethical and legal considerations

As we've discussed in Chapter 5, AI monetization comes with various ethical and legal considerations, including privacy, bias, and transparency. It's critical to address these considerations upfront, through practices such as data anonymization and fairness testing, to ensure that your AI initiatives are compliant and ethical.

- Monitor and optimize AI performance

Finally, it's important to monitor and optimize AI performance continuously to ensure that it's delivering the intended business outcomes. This can include tracking key performance indicators (KPIs) such as customer satisfaction, revenue growth, and cost savings, and making adjustments as needed.

Final Thoughts

In conclusion, AI offers tremendous potential for driving profits in businesses of all kinds. However, successful AI monetization requires a combination of technical expertise, domain knowledge, and a deep understanding of customer needs and expectations. By following the actionable steps outlined in this book and being mindful of the ethical and legal considerations of AI monetization, businesses can unlock the full potential of AI for driving profits and stay competitive in a rapidly evolving market.

"To my loving wife, son and beautiful daughter."

ABOUT THE AUTHOR

Kwame Joseph

Kwame Joseph is a licensed realtor with over 10 years of experience in the real estate industry. He has won numerous awards for his exceptional work in the field and has become a respected name in the industry. Born in Georgetown, Guyana, Kwame immigrated to the United States at the age of 8. Throughout his life, he has faced many challenges, but he has always been determined to succeed.

www.ingramcontent.com/pod-product-compliance
Lightning Source LLC
LaVergne TN
LVHW010040070326
832903LV00071B/4535